# ALL THE FEELINGS

*Hella Dramatic Monologues
for Thespians of a Teen Age*

M. F. A. Levine, MFA\*

\* Master of Feeling Arts

Written by
**MIKE LEVINE**

Edited and Designed by
GEOFFREY GOLDEN
AMANDA MEADOWS

Cover Art:
"Theater" by David Lopez from Noun Project
"Theater" by Max Hancock from Noun Project

ISBN-10: 1-942099-08-8

ISBN-13: 978-1-942099-08-6

First Edition: July 2016

devastatorpress.com

PRINTED IN ~~OFF-OFF-OFF-OFF-BROADWAY~~ KOREA

*All the Feelings* is a work of satire. All names and characters who appear in this parody
are fictional and satirical representations. Any similarities to *All the Feelings* creations
and living persons are purely coincidental. Also, don't sue us. We have no money!

*To my theatre teachers, Christine Farrell and Andy Spear,*
*whom I did not need but enjoyed my time with nevertheless.*

# PRAISE FROM REAL LIFE ACTORS

"This book will make you the hit of your high school thespian conference, impressing tech-theatre girls wearing faerie wings and drama teachers with uncontrollable rage issues alike!"

–DC Pierson, Author of *Crap Kingdom*, "Mayor" in *Bye Bye Birdie*, Mountain Pointe Theatre Company '02

"As both an actor and an acting teacher, I alone understand the importance of listening solely to myself while simultaneously demanding others listen only to me. This book is a reminder that feelings are weapons, and weapons, as I imagine the famous educator Maria Montessori would have said, 'exist only as a means to slay your audience with a fresh soliloquy.' Well done, Levine!"

–Dr. Matt Gourley, *Drunk History*

"If this book had existed when I was starting out, God knows where I would have ended up."

–James Urbaniak, *The Venture Bros* & *Difficult People*

"There are two things I can't stand: humor books, and one person shows. That said, dibs on the one person show of this humor book. I CALLED DIBS!"

–Laura Silverman, *Bob's Burgers*

# TABLE OF CONTENTS

Introduction ...................................................... 1

Q & A ............................................................. 2

Glossary .......................................................... 4

12 Things You *Don't* Need for Your Monologue ..................... 7

3 Things You *Do* Need for Your Monologue ......................... 8

Acting Exercises for One! ......................................... 9


Beginner:

    Twenty-one Thousand Questions (Curious) ..................... 12

    The Ultimate Prank (Mischievous) ........................... 14

    Who's in Therapy Now, Dr. Schwartzman? (Smug) .............. 16

    The Shocked Jock (Angry) ................................... 18

    I'm Your Daughter, Dammit (Frustrated)...................... 20

    Maybe I Should Have Tried at All (Regretful) ............... 22

    Everyone's Feeling Alive Without Me (Bummed) ............... 24

    When Life Gives You Mons Pubis (Shaved) .................... 26


Intermediate:

    Wouldn't You Hit It? (Betrayed) ............................ 28

    Shalom Shame, Shalom Redemption (Guilty) .................. 30

    You Can Go with This Guy... (Heroic) ...................... 32

    I Like to Think We Taught You (Righteous) ................. 34


Advanced:

    Smack Palace (Drugged) .................................... 36

    The Love Letter (Hopeful) ................................. 38

    The Overnight Mission (Paranoid) .......................... 40

    When I'm Dancing (Sensual) ................................ 42

    No Resolution (Shell-shocked) ............................. 44

    Don't Get Trundle Popped (Tough) .......................... 46

    Babies Don't Give Themselves Up (Proud) ................... 48

# INTRODUCTION

Congratulations, young actor! Simply by picking up this book, you have already felt something.

Before we dive into the marvelous world of monologues, an introduction. I'm M. F. A. Levine, MFA – which stands for Michael Francis Alberto Levine, Master of the Feeling Arts. In my adventures in the theater, I've written one-act plays, sketches, skits, routines, scenes, and two-act plays – often to completion! Because of my uncompromising passion and unwillingness to revise my material, I've been kicked out of ensembles, troupes, groups, schools, workshops, tech booths, rehearsals, and theater lobbies. I've had so many problems with collaboration, it took me a while to identify the common factor: Other people!

Once I found myself alone, that's when I really found myself. Even though I didn't go solo voluntarily, it led me to the last pure art form: Monologues! If you're reading this and silently mouthing the words to yourself, practicing gestures with your free hand, you're probably on the same path. I needed to write characters at my level of intelligence and maturity, and you needed something to read out loud to hear your own voice. We both really needed this book.

As a young actor, you don't need any secret acting trick or magical drama amulet to make a great performance. I'm here to show you that you had the power of *All the Feelings* inside yourself this whole time! No acting school or technique can teach you what you already have bursting forth at all times. You don't have to know *anything* to feel *everything*!

Let's get started!

*It's pronounced Levine.

# Q & A

*Before we get started, why don't we do something* **bold** *and* **nontraditional** *and* **start** *with a Q & A?*

**Q: What is a monologue?**
A: A better question would be: What *isn't* a monologue?

**Q: Okay, what *isn't* a monologue?**
A: A Scene. Scenes are awful. Scenes are when two or more actors fight for attention, forcing the audience to ping-pong back and forth like some sort of small-scale tennis match. No audience wants the responsibility of directing their own focus. In fact, the most collaborative forms of theatre (i.e. improv) are the least dignified.

**Q: So then, a monologue is a scene with one actor?**
A: Yeah, kinda.

**Q: Why do young actors need monologues?**
A: Monologues need young actors! It's a beautiful codependent relationship. Young people have, on average, **way** too many feelings. Monologues are the purest, loudest, and most direct way to express them.

**Q: Why get monologues from a book? Aren't there monologues on the Internet?**
A: No, there are no monologues on the Internet. There are other monologue books, but none of them have all the feelings. You wouldn't buy a periodic table with *most* of the elements, would you?

**Q: Can these monologues be performed by people of any race?**
A: Oh, I didn't even think about that. Probably not?

**Q: Are these monologues in order, from beginner feelings to the hardest feelings to feel?**

A: Yes, yes they are!

**Q: What is a feeling?**

A: Now you're getting somewhere. Why don't we start by defining everything *else* in the Theatre?

**Q: Wait, we're just getting started now?**

A: Well, I am. I'm afraid you won't make it out of this section alive.

**Q: Why do I feel so dizzy? What's in this drink?**

A: I'm sorry, but this is a monologue book. I couldn't allow any more dialogue. Someone had to go, and I'm the one with the combination to the poison safe.

**Q: Huuuuch...gaalluhhkk.....blurrch?**

A: Yes, blurrch. Shhh, it's all over now. Let's get to those monologues!

*Throughout this book you'll find T. I. P. S. (To "Insure" Proper Soliloquies). Read them, practice them, cherish them, and be willing to die for them if necessary. Is that overdramatic? Actually, that's a trick question. There's no such thing as "overdramatic" in the theatre.*

**T. I. P. S.**

# GLOSSARY

*Before we get to those monologues, you might want to learn a few common theatre terms to drop into casual conversation and let everyone know you're part of a special secret society of performers.*

**AD LIB** – Short for "additional liberation," this means adding extra words to the script to make room for more feelings. The monologues in this book do not require ad-libbing, unless you have finished reading the entire piece and no one has stopped you.

**AUDITION** – An audition is when an actor asks other people for permission to express themselves. You don't need permission; you should live your whole life like an audition. Make every day a performance and let the opportunities come to you!

**BEAT** – Hitting your own chest to drive a point home. Any time stage directions say [beat], make sure to really sock it to yourself, like a mountain gorilla or Celine Dion. This is a great way to bring pathos to an audience who might already feel like hitting you.

**BLOCKING** – Any movement you make onstage to ensure you're at the exact center of attention. This may not be the center of the stage, so walk around a bunch until you feel comfortable.

**COLD READ** – Reading a script out loud for the first time. It's important to be gentle and take your time. You never forget your first time with a script, even if you're not looking to get attached.

**CUE** – A signal to begin speaking. In the English Theatre, cues are known as "lines."

**DIRECTOR** – Just another person trying to tell you what to do. You don't need them.

**DOWNSTAGE** – The direction from which an actor receives attention.

**ENTRANCE** – The moment you arrive onstage to entrance the audience.

**EXEUNT** – All actors leave the stage.

**EXIT** – Vulgar street slang for "exeunt."

**FEELING** – Where an emotion meets its host body. Feeling our feelings is the most important thing we humans do, whether it's feeling for someone who's down, or feeling up someone who's doing great. Much like autism and sexuality, feelings exist on a spectrum. This book contains all of the feelings, and any other feeling you may have heard of is some bootleg combination of the feelings herein.

**INDICATE** – Pointing with your face, words, or body.

**LINES** – Words fortunate enough to be spoken by an actor. In the English Theater, lines are known as "queues."

**NOTES** – Non-praise feedback. To be avoided at all costs.

**OFF BOOK** – Performing a script without having it tucked into your tights somewhere. Not recommended.

**PATHOS** – Using your feelings to make the audience feel more feelings.

**PROJECTION** – Speaking very loudly, or speaking as if you're talking to one of your parents. These skills work very well in tandem. The harder you feel, the louder you are. The louder you are, the harder you feel, so speak real loud and keep it real!

**PROSCENIUM ARCH** – A scenium arch for professional use.

**SCRIPT** – All the words onstage!

**STAGE** – All the world's a stage!

**THEATER** – An area to perform feelings in. A theater does not require walls or a ceiling, but a floor is always necessary. Only veteran actor TOM HANKS has performed without a floor, in the movie *Apollo Thirteen*.

**THEATRE** – The greatest feeling of all. An umbrella feeling that contains all of the feelings, much like this book!

**UPSTAGE** – Leaning away from an audience to draw them in. Also refers to an actor trying to get more attention than you, which is thankfully impossible in a monologue.

**WINGS** – The sides of the stage, which hold it firmly in place to prevent feelings from leaking out of the theater.

*Note: These are all partial definitions. In the theatre, everything has multiple meanings, even words. Especially words! Even the word "words" has multiple meanings. Sometimes it means "a bunch of words" and sometimes it means "just two words."*

# 12 THINGS YOU *DON'T* NEED FOR YOUR MONOLOGUE

*We're almost at monologue o'clock, but first let's throw out everything you DON'T need and remind ourselves of the only things you DO need!*

**12. Help from Anyone** – Monologues remove the most cumbersome aspect of working in the theater, collaboration. You don't need a director, teacher, or feedback of any kind. All you need are these words and all your natural, organic, free-range feelings. You are *more* than enough.

**11. Mom & Dad** – They might have brought you into this world, but they don't understand anything about it. Invite them to every performance so you can show them you don't need them at all.

**10. Food** – Many actors develop an unhealthy relationship with food, which is great because unhealthy relationships produce the most interesting feelings. An empty stomach leaves room for a chunky imagination.

**9. Fear** – Fear is a scab that keeps feelings from oozing to the surface and infecting other people. You don't need that protection. Scratch it off, hold it up to the light, and flick it away.

**8. Ideas** – Knowing is the opposite of feeling. You don't need to "know" any acting techniques or "have" any experience. Actors act, and any action you take is an act of acting.

**7. Ideals** – The only minds you should be changing belong to people who don't think you're talented. If you speak your ideals, you're no better than a lowly politician.

**6. Underwear** – See "When Life Gices You Mons Pubis," p. 26.

**5. Music** – Music is a coward's way of expressing himself, hiding behind a secret language of external instruments and chord digressions. The only "notes" an actor needs is on their performance, and you don't even need those!

**4. Dramaturgical Knowledge** – If you're playing a soldier in a war, you don't need to know if the war is Gulf, Vietnam, or "of the Worlds." Onstage, you're not on a need to know basis, you're on a need to *feel* basis!

**3. Money** – Other than this book, you don't really need to buy anything to make a monologue. Your own clothes can be a costume if you feel in them hard enough. Remember: Nothing is as necessary as you are.

**2. Pets** – Animals are incapable of human feelings, and are near-useless in a theater. They're notoriously hard to control, especially ones that are still alive.

**1. Shame** – The greatest actors don't have any.

## 3 THINGS YOU *DO* NEED FOR YOUR MONOLOGUE

**3. This Book** – Keep a copy in your backpack. If a feeling hits, you'll have the words to go with it!

**2. A Chair or Cube** – Chairs and cubes are the vertebrae of the backbone of theatre. Sit on them, stand on them, prop a leg up, or hold them over your head. The possibilities are fourfold!

**1. An Audience** – Stuff your show and show your stuff!

*Almost ready for those monologues? Nope! You're not warmed up yet!*

# ACTING EXERCISES FOR ONE!

*As an actor, you are your own instrument, a machine gun of feelings cleverly hidden inside a guitar case. Even the best instruments/guns need a little lubing and tuning now and again – if you're not feeling constantly inspired, try a few of these exercises to get back on track!*

**Trust Leans** – In collaborative theatre, they often do what is known as "Trust Falls," which combine the terror of falling with the banality of catching. This exercise is pure hooey, because the only person you really need to trust is yourself. To do a Trust Lean, begin by leaning against a wall. You're only on the step one, and already you look cool! Next, take one step away from the wall and lean on it again. Hold that pose for thirty seconds and trust that you look even cooler. Take another step away from the wall, then lean over again. It gets scarier, but you have to trust you look cool even if you fall on your face. That's what theatre is all about!

**The Mirror Game** – If a parent or teacher starts yelling at you, try to "mirror" their voice and movements exactly. It'll drive them nuts to be confronted with an exact copy of their greatest enemy – themselves! All of a sudden, they're a character in your play, and you've got the upper hand – as well as a brand new character! To do this alone, find the nearest mirror and mirror your own voice and movements exactly. It'll be a lot of fun to be confronted with an exact copy of your best friend – yourself!

**Zip Zap Huh?** – A new take on the pass-the-impulse group game "Zip Zap Zop," sometimes called "Flip Flap Flop" or "Hip-Hop/Rap." All you need is three nonsense words and seventeen full-length mirrors arranged in a circle. Throw your energy across the circle with a loud *zip!*, pass it to the next mirror with a *zap!*, and give a hearty *huh?* as you lose track of your impulse!

**Animal Morphs** – Remember that weird Kitty Kat phase you went through when you were three years old? Swiping at random objects, crawling on the floor, embarrassing your parents in front of company. It may have been your greatest performance to date! Get back to those glory days by acting like an animal of your choice. Consider the animal's perspective through all five senses, especially smell, and remember that all animals are colorblind. Spend a little time as this animal in public, then draw even more attention to yourself by "transforming" into someone who's acting like a different animal! For an extra challenge, try to think of new, crazy animal combinations, like a snake with legs or a spider with less legs!

**What Am I Doing?** – A variation on the popular improv game "What Are You Doing?" In this exercise, mime doing something like typing or brushing your teeth. Really get into it, strive to feel each bristle and keystroke. Ask yourself: What kind of toothpaste am I using? Has the letter G popped out of the keyboard again? Once you've fully committed to the activity, it may take fifteen to ninety minutes before you start to feel ridiculous. Once you do, shout "What Am I Doing?" and begin a new activity.

**One Word Story** – Standing in the center of a circle, tell an original story out loud. But here's the catch – you can only say one word at a time! No pausing or interrupting yourself. If you mess up, you have to start over. (But if no one's around, who's going to know?)

**Self-Association** – Here's another fun word game for Player Number One (that's you!). Think about a word that has nothing to do with you. It may take a few minutes, but stick with it. Say your word is "Salmon." Think hard about what you and that word have in common to find your new word. For example, a Salmon is a rebel who swims upstream, just like you! Now you have the word "Rebel," which describes you.

Connect that word back to a new word that has nothing to do with you, like "Ugandan." Relate that back to yourself, because like Uganda, you are "Mysterious." Repeat until you've used all your words. Directing your thoughts away from yourself is a great way to bring them right back home!

**What's in the Box?** – Act like someone just handed you a box. It can be a big box, a small box, or any of the other sizes. (For example, medium.) But this is no ordinary box – inside is a present for you! What is it!? Greedily tear off the ribbon and wrapping with your hands and teeth, and open the box. Like most presents, whatever's inside is terribly disappointing. Look up at the "other person" who gave it to you, and try to thank them for it while hiding your disappointment. Then turn around just as someone else hands you a new box – inside is a present for you! What is it!?

**The Floor Is Lava!** – Pretend the floor is lava, and you've got lava-proof boots so it's no big deal. Strut around as everyone around you burns to death. This is a great confidence booster. The color of your boots is up to you!

*Now that you've had your Q's A'd, learned a few terms, thrown out everything you don't need, brought in everything you do, and tuned your fine self up, it's time for* All the Feelings. *Let's feel this.*

# TWENTY-ONE THOUSAND QUESTIONS

*For: Beamish boy, 13 years of age.*

 **CURIOUS** *is a feeling that's like being tickled – except you don't know where those fingers are coming from! To play curious, arch one eyebrow (at a time!) and look up to the sky as much as possible. That's where answers come from!*

*[sits cross-legged on the floor]*

I think about a lot of stuff when I'm alone in my room. Big questions, about life and the galaxy. Like, where do you go when you die? Is there life on other planets? And why doesn't Shannon Meckler love me?

I guess I just have a natural curiosity, I'm pretty profound. Why do bad things happen to good people? For that matter, why do good things happen to bad people? Why don't good people love other good people? Because they're not tall enough? Because they can't grow a moustache just yet? *[shrugs]* I just let my mind wander all over the place.

*[leaps to feet, paces around]* Is space infinite? Are humans the most advanced form of life? Is time travel possible, and if so can you change your past to make someone else part of your future? Are there other dimensions? Like maybe one where the sky is green, and everyone loves who they're supposed to? That'd be pretty crazy!

Are humans in control of their actions? That's one I think about a whole lot. Like, for example, did Shannon Meckler consciously decide I'm not her type? Because I think I am, and it's my word against hers. Maybe she's just confused. Like maybe there's outside factors that made her not notice me. Yeah, maybe she has unrealistic expectations about boys, and it's not her fault. If I got a bunch of muscles and found a way to take my shirt off at school, would that change things? Hmm.

I don't know if anyone else thinks about this kinda junk, so I mostly keep it to myself. Nobody knows if God has a plan for us, that's his business. Or hers, wow. *[grabs head, it's all so crazy]* Whoa, hold on: What if Shannon Meckler *is* God? She sure is pretty enough. What if she's testing my faith!? If so, I'm gonna ace that test!

Sometimes I'll write these philosophical thoughts down in my journal, sometimes I'll whisper them into my pillow. I never get any answers, but I guess that's what life's all about. I can't help but wonder, I'm so curious! I should put all these questions into a book, or maybe a thirty-paragraph email that I send from an anonymous account so it can't be traced back to me. I gotta put all these thoughts somewhere!

*[exeunt]*

**Make Those Silences Loud!** *Silence is the actor's worst enemy, so cram as much meaning as you can into every single one. And just because you're not talking, it doesn't mean you shouldn't be making noise. Breathe heavily, cough, sniffle, or let out a powerful low growl between words. Even if you're not making face noises, you can stomp around or point at things. Get those pauses pregnant!*

**T. I. P. S.**

# THE ULTIMATE PRANK

*For: Snotty male, 14 years of age.*

 **MISCHEVOUS** *is another fun feeling. Smiling like a devil while acting like an angel lets you express all two sides of the human experience. Ain't you a stinker? You are!*

*[strides in, thumbs in overall straps]*

I just love pullin' pranks. Nothin' makes me happier than really confusing someone, so's they don't know which way is up or down. I got some buddies that help me out. We're a prank crew, and I'm the leader because I come up with the best ones. I guess I got a sixth sense – one for pranks!

Most of our pranks are on our Social Studies teacher, Mr. Balmanian. This one time, we wrapped his car in double-sided tape. He couldn't get the tape off without getting himself stuck! It's that sweet layer of irony that makes it really funny. And we never got caught!

This other time, we ordered fifty pizzas to his house. Getting food you didn't even order is hella ironic. We were watching from across the street, and we couldn't hear exactly what he was saying to the delivery guy, but it was something like "Oh hey, these pizzas aren't for me!" "Sir, you gotta pay for these!" "Duhh, okay!" I still can't believe he coughed up the dough, then walked them straight to the dumpster! That was the second layer of irony: You're supposed to eat food, not throw it out! Wasting food is hilarious. He even let the delivery guy keep the change. What a bunch of mischief!

*[runs downstage, whispers]* This other other time, we disconnected the phone in his office, turned the lights off, and locked him inside over a long weekend. Oh man, it was sweet. We put a night vision camera in the corner, and the footage was hilarious! He spent thirteen hours walking in a circle and crying. It's like, walk in another shape, dude! The best part is, when the police found him and let him out, he was shaking so bad he couldn't say one word!

But my real masterpiece was the time we, get this, told him his wife died in an industrial accident. He didn't believe us, because we pulled all those other pranks in the same week. The real ironic thing was, you guessed it, she really had died! So he gets confirmation from the police, and we scored two pranks in one! You should have seen his face, he was like "Durr, I don't know what's real!" He was so shocked, he literally went into shock. He's headed to the hospital right now. And I'm headed to the prank hall of fame!

When you think about it, the truth is the ultimate prank. No backsies on that! *[cracks up for thirty seconds]* I hope they don't look into what caused the accident too hard, because then the prank would be on me and the boys. And we hate getting pranked!

*[skips offstage]*

---

**T. I. P. S.**

**Plan on Being in the Moment!** *Let's say you're onstage and your butt starts itching, or gets more itchy. This might take you "out of the moment" – UNLESS your character's butt itches too! Prepare a quick backstory where your character didn't do a great job wiping, zipping up, or tucking everything in. You'll go from embarrassing pants accident to brave pants CHOICE in no time!*

# WHO'S IN THERAPY NOW, DR. SCHWARTZMAN?

*For: Female smartass, 16 years of age.*

 **SMUG** *is a really fun feeling. Being smug is like having an inside joke with the audience – that everyone else is dumb! As a teen, you already suspect you're better than everyone, and now you can prove it just by stepping onstage! Put the MUG in SMUG by winking at the audience with your whole face. A mouth wink is called a smirk, and a nose wink is called a snit.*

*[brings out a chair, flips it around in the coolest way, and faces the audience sitting in it backwards.]*

Oh hello, Dr. Schwartzman. Yes, I will have a seat. I've been coming into your office for a few weeks now, right? I bet you think you've got me all figured out. Well today's therapy session is going to be a little bit different.

Last time I was here you told me to bring in three objects that expressed how I feel, but boy did I outsmart you. Really flipped the script. *[takes items out of backpack]* See, I brought a diploma, a box of tissues, and a notebook. And I got one question for you.

WHO'S IN THERAPY NOW, DR. SCHWARTZMAN, WHO'S IN THERAPY NOW?

Oh, how the tables have turned. Now I'm not undergoing therapy in your office, you're undergoing therapy in my office. Now I'm the smug one. And after I chew you up and spit you out, mind-wise, you're going to need even more therapy. See how you like it.

*[dumb therapist voice]* So, Greg, how's work going? Did enough kids cry in

your office for you to hit your quotas? Is it fun, profiting off the pain of innocent adolescents? Do you go home and laugh at all our problems with your poker buddies?

What's going wrong in *your* life? What are *you* afraid of? Let's see a chart of everything *you* ate this week. Is that enough for a growing *jerk*? Are you scared one of *your* patients will figure out you're a fraud? What's your relationship like with *your* mother? Do you think that applies to *your* problems today? [*back to cool teen voice*] Spoiler alert, it totally does. See, anyone can do this. I'm beating you at your own mind games, and you're speechless.

Do you want to see my notes? You never show me yours, but I'm not afraid to show you mine. I'm not a coward who hides behind a desk and glasses. [*dumb therapist voice*] Greg Schwartzman is an incompetent shithead who thinks everyone has an eating disorder just because they get dizzy sometimes. His breath smells like what I had to figure out was nicotine gum, so thanks for the lesson, Doc. Oh, and he's probably super impotent. Case closed.

Before you admit defeat, I'm going to have to cut you off there, because it looks like we're out of time.

I'll leave the tissues. [*shoves chair over, walks out*]

[*exeunt*]

# THE SHOCKED JOCK

*For: Oafish male, 16.5 years of age.*

 **ANGRY** *is when your feelings go from their usual simmer to a full-blown boil. It's is a Thanksgiving feast of feeling — there are many sides to it! Screaming, stomping, swearing, anything that starts with the letter S is a great way to display anger. Bonus points if you burst a blood vessel in your neck or face!*

*[enters chest first, holding bandana]*

Well guys, this is it. It's halftime, we're down by a bunch of points, and I just got word from Coach Barlowe that the school just cut all the funding for Sports.

Calm down guys, stop yelling. It's not that bad. Turns out, it's even worse! *[rips off, throws bandana]* There's gonna be no more football team, no more baseball team, and no more girl sports. This is the last game we're ever going to play together, and we need to win it!

What's that? Why? Well, Coach said they had to relocate some money in the school's budget. He said the administration did some studies and the studies showed we don't need Sports anymore. The studies showed that people don't learn anything from Sports, that there's no real point, that we're just playing the same game over and over. But who did those studies, huh? Not the Sports department, that's for sure. I think this whole thing is a crap-load of BS. We're not in school to make studies, we're in school cause we're gladiators, warriors. I'm so angry! *[knocks chair over]*

I said to Coach, I said, "but Coach, Sports is a great way to learn life lessons!" He said the administration told him that life lessons weren't the same as real lessons. I said, "Huh?" He said he didn't know, then we got real confused and started shoving each other until we ran out of breath. Coach was real upset, but I was glad I could be there for him, so he'd have someone to shove. Now we all gotta be there for Coach, and give him some kind of victory.

Guys, you're all nodding in agreement and pumping your fists, but I think I might be even madder than everyone here! I got so many feelings about this. If only there was some other department at school I could use to express these feelings! But there probably isn't.

We gotta go out there, win that game, and prove a point. Sometimes being a hero means having the courage to do something that doesn't matter. We're taking a stand and showing the whole world we can get those points. We might have lost the war, but if we work together and get all of our guys to the other side and just one of us has the ball, we can WIN. THIS. BATTLE. Who's with me?

*[charges off, pumping fist]*

*[exeunt]*

**Score Some Focal Points!** *Some say you should focus slightly above the head of the person in the back row, but some are dead wrong. Look the person in the back row directly in the eye. Why are they sitting in the back? Were they late? Trying to sneak out early? What's their deal? If you need to stop your performance to ask these questions out loud, it will make you look very caring and professional.*

**T. I. P. S.**

# I'M YOUR DAUGHTER, DAMNIT

*For: Daughters of any gender, 15 years of age.*

 **FRUSTRATED** – *Your parents may tell you few things in life are fair, but you know the truth: Absolutely nothing in life is fair. This creates a deep well of frustration you can throw a bucket into anytime! To show frustration, clench your fists into little balls and clench your legs all the way up into your butt. Point everywhere with your clenched fists until you find who's at fault.*

Dad, I know you've got your headphones in and you can't hear me, but I've got some stuff to say. I know things have been tough since Mom left. I want to be here for you, I really do. But I'm your daughter, dammit. I'm your daughter. *[points to self]*

I'm not your friend. I know monogamy goes against every natural instinct humans have, and I know that sexually, you just can't be everything to your partner. But you *really* shouldn't have told me that. I wanted to find out on my own. It's hard to parse out the life lessons when you're talking about my mom. You told me her libido's been low since she's been on antidepressants, I didn't even know she was on them! That would have been nice to hear from *her*.

And I'm certainly not your lawyer. Just because I knew what a trial separation was and you didn't, that doesn't mean I know anything about custody law. You always said I was smarter than you, and I think that's really sweet, but maybe I'm not. Maybe we're both dumb. *[points to Dad and self]*

I'm not your bartender. Sure, it was cute when I was a kid and I'd bring you a "dwink," or crack open a beer, but now you're into this crafted cocktail stuff and I can't keep up. I don't know what a "botanical infusion" is, and I don't want to know! Let me hang on to my innocence for a few more years. I'm so frustrated!

I'm not your Rabbi. I don't know what God's plan is for you, I don't even know what God's plan for me is! I know I have the wisdom of a child, but you're supposed to have the wisdom of an adult!

I'm not your mother, either. She keeps asking about you, and you need to call her back. See, she's your parent, and she's supposed to help *you*. And you're supposed to help me. It goes oldest to youngest. I made a diagram to help you out, it's on the fridge. I'm your daughter, Dad. Just let me be your daughter, and also your personal chef. I made White Corn Polenta with Truffle Butter, once you come back to the real world it'll be waiting for you on the dinner table. I'll be waiting too, in the chair. *[points, walks offstage]*

*[exeunt]*

---

**Listening Hard Is Difficult!** *It's a well-known truth in the theatre that acting is the opposite of reacting. That's why there are two different words. Sometimes, even in a monologue, you will be forced to act as if someone else is speaking. What a chore! Instead of asking for a friend to pretend to listen to you in rehearsals – remember, you don't need anyone – imagine you are someone else listening to yourself. This way, you can play all the parts. Remember: There are no small parts, there is only one actor. And it's you!*

**T. I. P. S.**

# MAYBE I SHOULD HAVE TRIED AT ALL

*For: Goony male, 15 years of age.*

**REGRETFUL** – *As a teen, the worst thing that can happen to you is missing out on something. Regret is the stinging feeling of knowing you did. Regret is the opposite of smug, so instead of winking, try blinking with your whole face. Scrunch it up like you're squinting into the past to see where it all went wrong.*

*[speaks into a phone.]*

Hello? Tritch? Was that the beep? Am I doing this right? I've never left a voicemail before. You're not answering my texts and my hands got real tired, but I gotta talk to you, Tritch! I got some things I gotta say! I gotta! *[shakes fist at downstage sky]*

I've been going crazy bonkers since you broke up with me, but I figured some stuff out. I need you to know I'm sorry for the way I've always acted. I've been thinking about it, not too much, but it's still a lot of thinking for me. And it hurts! *[grabs scalp muscles, squeezes]*

I finally understand why you broke up with me. What I don't understand is, are you hearing this message later, like a podcast? Or are you hearing it right now? I don't know, I'm still learning. You gotta come back to me, so I can figure this out. Without you, I don't have a girlfriend!

You said I never tried, I never listened to you. And the crazy thing is, you were right. Well I'm ready now. I'm ready to try to listen, and I'm ready for you to listen to me try. Reply me on this voicemail, and I swear I'll listen to it right in front of you, all the way through.

I've been such an idiot. You texted me three times as often as I texted you, and all you got in return was a lowercase k. I could have capitalized it, I could have texted "OK," or even "O-K-A-Y." You're worth all four letters, Tritch. I regret so much. You deserve a guy who replies within 48 hours, and I can be that guy, I know I can. That's why I'm using this crazy voicemail technology, to show you I care. I don't care if I have to write something on paper with my own two hands. I'll do it.

Sometimes, you don't know what you've got until she says she's leaving, and you check your texts three days later and realize she really is gone. And it's shredding me up inside!

*[looks at phone, puzzled]*

Tritch, I just heard another beep, and I don't know what that means. I don't know what anything means without you! I'm talking my damn heart out, more talking than I've ever done all at once before. Tritch, I miss you. Without you, I'm not O-K-A-Y. I'm not ok. I'm not even k.

*[exeunt]*

**Dealing with Tech Goblins:** *Techies control the very light with which you get attention, and you'd think they'd be more grateful for it. Common sense would dictate that you should treat these black shirted (and hearted!) nerds with respect, but common sense has no place in the theater. Techies thrive off your contempt! Don't worry about taking it too far: The occasional mysteriously loosened spotlight falling on your head is worth the attention.*

**T. I. P. S.**

# EVERYONE'S FEELING ALIVE WITHOUT ME

*For: Long-faced male, 16 years of age.*

 **BUMMED** *is that "five more minutes" feeling of wanting to sleep in, but for some people it lasts all day! To play bummed, act as if you're 15 to 90 pounds heavier than you are. Try filling your pockets with rocks, which some people who are super bummed end up doing anyway!*

*[curls up on two chairs pushed together to resemble a bed, wraps self in a stage blanket]*

I wake up in the morning and feel no more alive. I don't know what's going to happen today, but I know it's going to be all my fault. I look at my phone and see the whole world is having a grand old time without me. I'm the most useless person in the world. I'm so bummed! *[slowly reaches arm out of blanket, falls onto floor]*

I get out of bed and somehow I'm already sitting on the floor. There's a story going around about a kid my age who invented an asthma inhaler that also works as sunglasses. Why couldn't I have invented that? Because I'm so tired. Why can't I have somehow already invented that? Sixteen and I'm already washed up. A super useless ultra failure.

*[rolls around on floor]*

I sit down in the shower and let failure rain down on my head. It's 11a.m. and humanity is way ahead of me. People are writing hit songs, getting promotions, finding their birth parents, inventing new medical devices that let kids with asthma feel cool for once. Not me. I'm a useless failure who's letting all the kids with asthma down.

I open the curtains, and the light is blinding. I could put on sunglasses but they're just the regular kind. If I wasn't such a human bummer, maybe I could think of some other use for them. A friend calls, but I don't feel like talking, so I don't pick up. Nobody cares about me. It's like...it's like the whole world is having a party and I wasn't invited. I'm not good at parties, or one on one, or by myself. There was a real party last night, and I was invited, but it was probably just as a joke. Everyone looks like they're having so much fun in the pictures, I bet they feel alive all day, every day. If I didn't feel so awful about myself, I could probably invent an orthopedic umbrella, or special shoulder pads for people with autism, or shin guards for diabetics. Shinsulin! Hey that's...that's not half bad. Maybe I'm not so bummed after all.

*[stands up, trips over blanket]*

*[exeunt]*

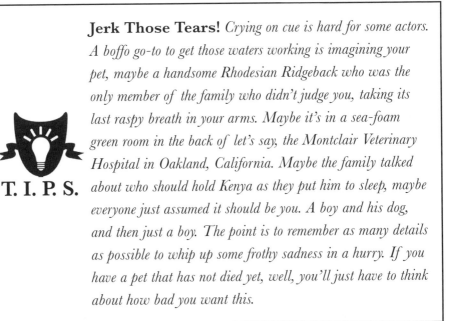

**Jerk Those Tears!** *Crying on cue is hard for some actors. A boffo go-to to get those waters working is imagining your pet, maybe a handsome Rhodesian Ridgeback who was the only member of the family who didn't judge you, taking its last raspy breath in your arms. Maybe it's in a sea-foam green room in the back of let's say, the Montclair Veterinary Hospital in Oakland, California. Maybe the family talked about who should hold Kenya as they put him to sleep, maybe everyone just assumed it should be you. A boy and his dog, and then just a boy. The point is to remember as many details as possible to whip up some frothy sadness in a hurry. If you have a pet that has not died yet, well, you'll just have to think about how bad you want this.*

**T. I. P. S.**

# WHEN LIFE GIVES YOU MONS PUBIS

*For: Lumpy male or female, 18 years of age.*

> **SHAVED** — *Shaving is what separates men from boys, and makes women's bodies look acceptable. Shaved feels simultaneously refreshing and vulnerable, like drinking a glass of lemonade that may have been poisoned. To convey shaved, expose as much of yourself to the audience as the laws in your state allow.*

*[floats lightly onstage, crouches into compact ball]*

Hello. We've met before. I am already a part of you. I am already in your pants. You don't think about me much, but maybe you should. I am Mons Pubis.

I am Mons Pubis, but you can call me Mons, because you are my friend. Your textbooks will tell you I'm the mound of fatty tissue over the pubic symphysis, yet I am so much more. I am a suprapubic dune, neither male nor female. I exist in a moment of unity. I am a prelude, an introduction, the shuddering gateway to vaginal secrets and penile announcements. *[swells into standing position]*

I am pubic. I am private. I am genital-adjacent. I go by many names. The Pleasure Parabola. Bikini Zone: Sector 1. Mound Town. Blueberry Hill. The Golden Arch. The Deep V. Launchpad of the Landing Strip. Mustache Rider. Arthur Monsarelli. The Mons.

I am not merely natural, I am nature itself. My secret garden grows lush and bushy, bushy and lush. I am Samson, less powerful without my hair. More powerful with it. But what's this? You, you whom I thought were my friend, have betrayed me. Oh, woe is me, woe is Mons!

I am so, so cold. *[shivers, slowly shrinks back down]* Why did you shave me? To fit in with your bikini models and sports champions? Because you were hoping a lover might see me tonight? Because no one will see me and you wanted to exert some measure of control? Because you were bored in the shower? Your double-headed razor burns both ways. If you betray me by going against my grain, I will have no choice but to grow hair into myself. I will go to war if need be. But I am not a fighter. I am an almost-lover.

I feel the icy kiss of your button fly rivets with every step you take. Why are you not wearing underwear? You are just asking for a rash. I am Mons Pubis, and I don't want to itch any more than you want to scratch me. I want to be kissed by a lover on their way downtown, and held with gentle pressure while they're there. I am the welcome mat at your front door, the cherry on top of the cherry.

I am a bumper, a buffer, a bouncer to your gentlest parts. I'm the bow on your greatest gift. Do not throw me away. Hold me close, keep me warm. Cup me. Pat me. Pet me. I am you and I am yours. I am Mons Pubis.

*[rolls off in a ball]*

*[exeunt]*

---

**Get Off, Get Off, Get Off Book!** *Even though reading aloud makes you look hella smart, at some point you might want to memorize these monologues and get "off the books," an embezzlement term that found its way into the theatre. The best way to memorize a monologue is to videotape yourself speaking into a tape recorder. That way, you have something to watch while you listen to yourself!*

**T. I. P. S.**

# WOULDN'T YOU HIT IT?

*For: Offended male, 16 years of age.*

 **BETRAYED** – *Look around you. Is anyone paying attention to you? If not, you've been betrayed! Betrayed is an advanced form of frustrated, where you know exactly who to blame. Pick one person who isn't paying attention to you, and focus that blame laser on them. Carry that onstage and project your betrayedness toward them as loudly as you can.*

What the hell, man? I thought we were friends. I thought we had each other's backs.

We've been friends since halfway through middle school. Dude, I know everything about you. I know your first boner was Moaning Myrtle from Harry Potter. I know you walked in on your cousin in the shower twice during the same shower. All the important stuff. And you know everything about me! You know *my* first boner was because of Natalie Portman's forehead. You know things got pretty serious with me and the gap between my mattress and box spring last summer. You even know how many inches I am. That's a sacred bond, bro. A bond you've gone and betrayed.

So when I lean over to you in history class, open my heart, and say, "Sarah Herman looks real boinkable in that tube top," as my friend, you've got several options. You can agree with me that she does look boinkable. How hard is that? You can tell me how you'd boink her, where you'd boink her, how you'd get her tube top off, maybe with your teeth. All interesting points of discussion. You don't even have to agree with me, I just want your participation. You can tell me whose melons you think would look even better in said tube top. You could tell me you wouldn't touch her with a ten foot pole. Any number of foot pole. I just want your opinion, because I care about you. You could even say nothing, just grunt. That'd be nice.

Heck, even if you went all gay, I could accept that, because you mean that much to me. In fact, it would be even more fodder for boink discourse! What's the dude equivalent of boobs? Is it biceps? Who's the most boinkable guy in class? Is it me? See, there's a back and forth there. It's discourse, dude!

But the one thing you can't ever, ever say is "Hey man, it's not cool to talk about chicks like that." Hey man it's *not cool* to talk about chicks like that? Hey man it's not cool to talk about chicks *like that?* You know who says stuff like that? Guys who aren't my friend, guys who I don't even recognize.

It's *always* cool to talk about chicks like that! How else are we gonna bond? If I share my innermost thoughts, and you can't even have the decency to tell me who you'd rather boink, well then we've got nothing to talk about.

*[walks halfway offstage, then back]*

Buddy.

*[exeunt]*

29

# SHALOM SHAME, SHALOM REDEMPTION

*For: Jewish boy, although Greek or Italian will do in a pinch, 14 years of age.*

 **GUILTY** *is the gift you give yourself after screwing up. You only have yourself to blame, which is super convenient – you're right in arms' reach! To show guilt, shoot a glaring look behind you, then snap your neck forward and wince at the present!*

Good afternoon, Temple Sinai Hebrew school. My name is Joseph Rosenbloom, some of you may already know me by reputation. I've been brought here to speak to you today by Rabbi Chester, to tell you about what happened to me.

Raise your hand if you're planning on having your Bar or Bat Mitzvah. Good, I see a lot of hands up. It's no problem if you don't want to for whatever reason. Raise your hand if you're looking forward to reading from the Torah in front of the whole congregation. Alright, I get it, you're nervous, I was too. Raise your hand if you're just looking forward to the party. Ha ha, okay, now we're getting honest. See, we're all friends here. Raise your hand if you're nervous that when you take the Torah out of its resting place in the ark, that you're going to drop it. I see some hands. Scary, right?

Raise your hands if you know someone who dropped the Torah in front of the whole congregation. Nobody? Well, you should all be raising your hands, because you know me. That's right. I'm the kid who dropped the Torah. I will carry this sin in my heart for the rest of my days. I can still remember the feeling of it slipping out of my hands, the thud as it hit the floor. Realizing what I had done, I immediately puked all over the Cantor and leaned on the curtain, which pulled down the eternal flame. One end of the Torah caught fire, and that's when I noticed the other end of the scroll rolling away. Trying to be the hero, I shoved the Rabbi aside and went chasing after it. He broke his wrist and hip. As it tumbled down the stairs and into the aisle, well, I couldn't catch it without stepping on it. And I couldn't step on it without tearing it. People were screaming, I turned around and the whole place was going up in flames. I made it out last with just my Torah portion clutched in my hand.

Now, we have a storied history of Temples burning down, but it's usually not by accident. So, so much can go wrong if you're not careful. Nobody was physically hurt besides the Rabbi, but as we watched the stained glass windows melt, I collapsed into a two-year shame coma. The doctors couldn't understand what was wrong with me until they found out what I did.

But my story does not end there. The whole congregation came together and told me it wasn't my fault, that it was an accident. They told me in shifts until I came out of my shame coma. They rebuilt the temple, and I went up and had my Bar Mitzvah, reading from the Torah with my hands behind my back. And by not giving up, I became a man in more ways than I ever thought I would.

Now I tour Hebrew schools across the country, sharing my story. This story is my *real* Torah portion. Don't end up like me. Keep your hands dry, throw a little chalk in your pockets if you need to, like a rock climber. Avoid rich foods before you take the bimah. If you drop something, let it fall. God will pick you back up.

*[exeunt]*

# YOU CAN GO WITH THIS GUY...

*For: White knight, 15 years of age.*

---

**HEROIC** – *Don't worry, you don't need to accomplish anything to feel heroic! To fake heroism (or female heroism), take an action figure and throw it against the wall. Adopt that pose and you'll feel heroic faster than a speeding super powered man!*

---

*[stands on a chair]*

Susie. Susie! SUSIE! I've got some things I need to say before I ask you out. Yes, right here, in the cafeteria during lunch, in front of everyone.

You've never even looked twice at me, Susie, but I've looked at you so many times. You never knew I existed, but I totally do. My name is Teb, and before you say one word, let me tell you everything about myself. I want you to understand who I am so you can also praise me for who I'm not. You see, I'm special, different. I'm not one of those guys, I'm one of this guy. This speech is going well so far.

Thing is, there's two types of men in the world, and I'm the good kind. Just like there's two types of women, and you're the beautiful kind. I'm not one of those guys who brags about how hard he is. You see, I'm one of those guys who brags about his six pack and forearms. So please, nobody interrupt me, because this is hard to express, even though I'm doing great at it and it's definitely working.

My whole life, all fifteen years, I've never been the guy who gets the girl. I'm not one of those pigs who plans two dates on the same night and lies to both of them. I'm one of those guys who has zero dates on one night and tells the truth to *himself*. I'm a rare breed, and I don't care if the whole school knows it. I'm not one of those guys who will ignore you, spurn you, reject you. One of those guys who will never be enough for you. No, I'm one of those brave men who dares to always be too much. Would you rather be starving or stuffed? Don't answer just yet. I'm here to save you from an army of those guys, many of them right here in the cafeteria, and all I ask in return is simply access to your body. You could change my whole life, right now. If you agree to go out with me, I can be the guy who sometimes gets the girl. I'm a gift to you, and you're exactly what I deserve.

*[steps off chair, walks slowly towards audience]*

You didn't know I existed, but now you know my true purpose. I'm going out on the flimsiest limb and taking a huge risk, and it's all super romantic. Everyone is looking at you, but most importantly, I am. Will you go out with me?

*[freezes before the audience sees the answer for maximum suspense!]*

*[exeunt]*

**T. I. P. S.**

**Defy Specificity!** *It's a known acting thingy that the more specific your performance, the more universally it connects to an audience. This makes no sense if you think about it for even five seconds. If your performance is too understandable, no one will be talking about you after the show, so vague it up a little with a mumble or a few unnecessary gestures.*

# I LIKE TO THINK WE TAUGHT YOU

*For: Two-shoed, goody female, 15 years of age.*

 **RIGHTEOUS** *is a feeling that's a lot like heroic, but much more advanced. Some might argue that they're the exact same feeling. Here's a tip: Don't worry about it!*

*[mimes closing door]*

Oh hey Mr. Morris, what are you still doing in your office? Graduation is in fifteen minutes!

*[turns chair around backwards, sits down]*

Actually, I'm glad you're here, I have something I need to tell you. It's been a pretty crazy senior year, right? Homecoming, winter formal, prom. It's been a wild ride. You made Teacher of the Year, I made Valedictorian. That's a funny word, valedictorian. Comes from Latin, means I'm the smartest in my class. Which is why I'm the only one who knows what you've been up to. Everyone's favorite English teacher has been scamming us all year.

That's right, I'm onto you. I'm onto your scheme. You see, you're supposed to be teaching us, but this whole time we've been teaching you! It's not fair, and it ends today.

Too shocked to respond? Fine, I'll continue. Remember when Diego was reading his love poem to the class, and you broke down crying? You told us all about your problems at home, and we all told you not to give up. Everyone thought you were breaking down the barriers between teacher and student, showing yourself as fully human. But it was something far more sinister. You were using us as bootleg therapy! What's that worth? Probably a whole lot more than knowing sonnet structure.

We've been writing our hearts out all year, really connecting as a group of teens who couldn't be more different, and you've been sitting on your fat ass reaping the benefits of our juicy life knowledge! Chandon taught you that someone who's angry is probably just hurting and doesn't know what to do. Rachel taught you about Karma, and Navya taught you not to believe everything Rachel says about Karma. Becky B. taught you that everyone is special, until Becky C. taught you we're all the same on the inside. We taught you the latest dances, cool slang, and that you're only as young as you feel. We helped you get your groove back, but I'm starting to suspect... maybe you never had a groove in the first place.

And what did we learn from you, huh? To start an essay in a larger context, gradually get more specific using concrete examples, then return to the larger context at the end? We could have looked that up online. We're your students, not your life coaches. The charade ends today.

*[whips a piece of paper out of her pocket dramatically.]*

Here's a little math for you, I know it's not your department. Thirty life coaches at a hundred dollars an hour, times 150 hours in class comes to $450,000. That's right, we're billing you. Learning is supposed to be a one-way street, Mr. Morris. I had to figure that out myself, because I sure didn't learn it from you. So now you know what happens when you mess with the Valedictorian. And that's the last thing I'm ever going to teach you. Class dismissed.

*[exeunt]*

# SMACK PALACE

*For: Skeevy-looking female, 17 years of age.*

 **DRUGGED** *is a feeling you shouldn't have too much experience with, but if you do, I won't snitch. To get a sense of the feeling, spin around until you almost fall down, then run straight forward into a wall. I won't snitch about that either.*

Anyway, I have a drug problem. I've been chased by The Amber Goblin since I was thirteen years old. I've ruined my life, my family's life, lost all my friends, and disgusted countless strangers.

Call the stuff whatever you want: Flicka, Worm Starch, Irish Grape, Sweet Lady Grout, The Devil's Septum, Charlie Parkour, Liquid Flannel, Stork Cracklins, Puff Paint. Those are just marketing terms for drug pushers to sucker you in, get you hooked. You think you're having fun, but then you find yourself in an alley trying to trade the academic credit from your internship for just one more hit of Bloom County.

But you don't want to hear about how I destroyed my life, you want to know what it feels like, don't you? *[points at audience member.]* Don't you? *[points at another audience member.]* Anyone can tell you how your life gets ruined, but no one tells you how good it feels. I've thought about it a lot, because it's all I ever think about.

*[rolls out blackboard]*

Take the feeling of your first kiss, and raise it to the power of your first orgasm. That's just for starters. You want to add the smell of a baby's head right after it rains, divided by the square root of finding ten dollars in an old jacket.

You vultures don't care that not a single one of my friends can look me in the eye anymore. You don't want to hear about how I made my mom cry so hard her earrings fell out. You just want to multiply all that by, and this is in parenthesis, the tightest hug from your grandma minus all the old lady smells. Close those parenthesis, and multiply that by the intensity of looking directly into a solar eclipse to the exponential power of the taste of a buttery baked potato so hot it would have burned you a split-second earlier.

Don't think about the hours I spent on the floor, thinking there were bugs under my skin when they were only on the outside. Just subtract every fear, every worry, every itch you ever had. Subtract doubt, subtract shame, subtract your social security number and where you left your keys. That's what it feels like, and I'm telling you, it's not worth it.

I needed all that just to feel normal. Now I don't know what normal is. I've blown out my pleasure receptors, so making love feels like bumping into a sliding glass door, and bumping into a sliding glass door feels like nothing at all.

I really thought drugs were the solution to all of my problems, but they just gave me more problems, as well as a drug problem. You don't want to end up like me. And it's not too late. For you, anyway. *[points at audience member, the one from before]* And you. *[points at other audience member, the other one from before]*

*[exeunt]*

# THE LOVE LETTER

*For: Doe-eyed female, 14 years of age.*

 **HOPEFUL** *is the dumbest of all the feelings, by far. It's tricky because it requires you to forget everything you know about the world being a crock of BS. Hope is a buoyant lightness that comes with thinking anything will work out fine. To show hope, open up every part of your body above the waist. If you start feeling stupid, you're on the right track!*

My cousin got a love letter from the president last week. No, not THAT kind of love letter. Let me explain. When you find the one, like THE one person you're supposed to be with for the rest of your life, you get an official letter from the White House. It's real hard to find anyone to get along with, much less true love, so it's a big deal, and it deserves recognition at the federal level. She even let me copy it! Here's what it says:

"Dear Citizen,

Congratulations on the monumental occasion of finding your soulmate!

You have defied the odds, opened your heart to the universe, and were rewarded with a romantic partner perfectly suited to you. With this accomplishment, you are now a complete person, and you have secured your place in the American History of Love.

You are now one of the rare citizens who completely understands what love is, and more importantly, who to get it from. You have solved the world's oldest problem, and now it is your responsibility to go forth and help others. Tell all your friends, coworkers, and cousins that if you found the one, they can too. Even if you don't think they ever will, it's good to give them a little hope. You could make up a story, or just give them this letter. It's the merciful thing to do. One day in this great nation every couple will have found each other, and on that day we will truly know peace.

As you reflect on your accomplishment, we hope you are filled with pride in your success. Please enjoy getting married and having babies without ever second-guessing yourself.

Signed,

The President of the United States of North America"

I mean, wow! I can't wait to find someone who loves me for me and get confirmation that I'm not wasting my time loving them back. All I got is this letter from the mayor saying I've been frenching all the wrong boys.

*[exeunt]*

 **Dumb It Downstage!** *A great way to keep your character "in the moment" is to make them "as dumb as possible!" Remember the acronym KISASS: Keep It Stupid,* **T. I. P. S.** *And Simple, Schmuck!*

# THE OVERNIGHT MISSION

*For: Bookish female, 13 years of age.*

 **PARANOID** – *Just because you're feeling paranoid, it doesn't mean the audience is going to get it. Paranoid is hard to get across, because you're already in your safe space: onstage! To show paranoia, bug your eyes out like bugs, and roll them around, like pillbugs!*

*[speaks into tape recorder]*

Space date: June 9th, 3069. I find myself on an alien planet, the likes of which I've never seen before. The ground here is made from a non-linoleum substance, some sort of shaggy, carpet-like material. The air here is strangely transparent, and seems to contain no tobacco smoke whatsoever. This bizarre environment bears no resemblance to my home...planet.

I have been summoned here on a diplomatic ritual known as a "Sleepover" by an ambassador who goes by the name of Craig. Craig clearly wants to strengthen relations between our species, he does not suspect I am here on a secret fact-finding mission to find facts. I have all my tools at my disposal, such as my tape recorder, extra batteries, and absorbent astronaut underwear.

The most disturbing thing I have observed by far is the behavior of the elders toward one another. They communicate in a strangely even tone, and with gestures that contain neither hitting nor throwing. I can't make sense of it. There is also an infant here that seems to be getting as much attention and care as the television, if not more. Something is very wrong here.

I have locked myself in this planet's bathroom, and even in here my findings are disturbing. The natural flora and fauna of mold and fungus one would normally find in a bathroom have been wiped out, perhaps by some sort of natural disaster. The medical supplies have been depleted, I see no uppers, downers, or diet pills. Instead I see scented soap shaped like seashells. Chilling. I've heard rumors that there is a second bathroom, that seems impossible. Maybe the other bathroom is a decoy, or maybe this...

*[There is a knock at the door.]*

Just a minute!

*[whispers]*

This may be my final transmission, as I'm being summoned downstairs for some sort of "Family Game Night." Clearly I'll be enduring a barbaric trial by combat, but it is unclear whether or not I will survive. End transmission.

*[exeunt]*

---

**One Small Step to Making the Space Yours!**
*A big problem for actors is other people claiming to "own" the theater space. They might have the lease, they might have the keys, but the actors are the ones who truly own the stage. To make the space yours, perform this secret acting ritual: Lick your finger and touch every surface. You now have "drama dibs!"*

**T. I. P. S.**

# WHEN I'M DANCING

*For: Jezebel, 18 years of age.*

**SENSUAL** – *Some of the nicest feelings come from feeling yourself. When the feelings in your swimsuit area spread across your sweatsuit area, that's sensual! To show sensuality, keep one hand on your body, and make "come hither" motions with your other hand and eyebrows. (Hither means "quickly!")*

*[dances onstage, then freezes]*

When I'm dancing, I forget about everything else. I don't know what my name is or what day of the week it is, or what time the dance center closes. It's just me and the music. We're friends, with benefits.

I start with my finger and press play. If the song isn't enough, I'll use two figures to skip to the next track. I let the sounds into my hands, a little jazz, a little tap. Then I let it roll into my arms. Arms are underrated in dance, sometimes I'll cut my elbows loose for fifteen to ninety minutes.

Next I let it into my chest, the music beating on and my heart beating off *[beat]* to the rhythm. Sometimes the music picks up the pace, and I'm like, slow down tiger, I'm just getting warmed up. But when I really get into it, I don't know who's in charge. You see, I never dance with a partner. The music is my partner, and he's a real good listener, if you know what I mean. It's all *very* sensual.

My legs come in last, and boy do they steal the show. The music doesn't care if I've shaved recently, or if my feet stink. The music's nasty like that. Sometimes the music will try to put my legs behind my head, and even though my legs don't stretch like that, I love that the music keeps trying new things. You can't just do the same moves over and over, it gets routine. When I'm dancing, there's no such thing as 5,6,7,8 – any of the numbers. What's inside me can't be choreographed, or contained in step, shimmy, kick-ball-change. There are no rules. I use up the whole space, and it uses me. I wear shoes for protection, even though it feels way better without them. Remember: When you take the floor, you're dancing with everyone that ever danced there. I try not to think about it. I try not to think at all. I whip myself into a frenzy, dive into the music, roll around in it, swim through it, until my white leotard turns black and the dance floor is spotless. It's so sensual!

Once the music has gotten into my hair and my head and my neck and my chest, my thighs and my toes, I let the music into the second most secret, sacred part of me: My mons pubis. I never let the music go all the way, I'm saving myself for a recital. Once the music gets into my pubic mound, there are no more rules, no laws. I forget about space and gravity. I don't know where I started bleeding from, don't know why my elbows hurt so much. Then, as quickly as it started, the music is finished. It's always too soon, but I try not to let on that I'm disappointed. Six minutes is pretty good for an extended remix. I want to stay and do it again, but instead I find my street shoes and shuffle my way outside with a whole new rhythm.

*[takes a few deep, loud breaths.]*

*[dances offstage]*

*[exeunt]*

# NO RESOLUTION

*For: Bedraggled female, 14 years of age.*

**SHELL-SHOCKED** *is an outdated diagnosis, but it's also a very advanced feeling! Shell-shocked is like wearing a list of everything bad that's ever happened to you – on your face! In fact, why not grab a washable marker and do just that!*

Mrs. Grimphauser, I'm retiring from my tour of duty. Go ahead and mark me as absent, without leave. I quit. *[takes lollipop out of pocket]*

I've been a conflict resolution volunteer for one and three quarter years, and I've seen too much. I've seen conflicts you wouldn't believe, the best friendships of my generation torn apart over stickers, barrettes, the good kickball. Kids calling each other names you won't find in any dictionary. I can't take it! I'm so shell-shocked!

*[tries to unwrap lollipop, hands are shaking too hard]* I've seen a girl crying, holding her snipped-off ponytail, trying to reattach it to the back of her head. I've seen cliques rise and fall in the twenty minutes between first and second periods. Kids, stuffed into lockers like old sweatshirts. I can pull them out, but they never leave the lockers in their mind.

You got me involved in conflicts I had no business being in, just so your administration could say they ran a tight ship. We're out here on the front lines, just so you can what, have a break? I've memorized acronyms no kid should have to. *[speaking robotically]* SNAFU – Sensitivity iNcourages A Friendly Understanding. FUBAR – Friends Understand, Bullies Always Ridicule. JAGHOLE – Justice Attacks

44

Grievances Head On, Loves Everyone. When I can't sleep at night, I run them over and over in my head. I bet you sleep pretty well, in your cushy teacher's lounge, counting your wages. And what the heck is a "Respectrum?" No one will tell me, and it's on all of our shirts!

Where does it end, Mrs. Grimphauser!? Not when the bell rings, that's second group lunch. Not when the day's over, they just come back tomorrow! Not next year, there's just going to be another crop of third graders, another stinky tide of He Saids and She Saids. Well I'm saying *[beat, then screams]* ENOUGH! IT ENDS WITH ME!

I'm sorry to use my outside voice, but that's just how my insides feel. Back in basic training, you taught us to use "I" statements: I feel BLANK when you BLANK and I think you should BLANK. Well, *I* feel burned out, when *you* put me on yet another tour of duty, and *I think you should* let me just have lunch. How can I make my own friendships if I'm always fixing others? I gotta get out of here, gotta turn in my sash. This is one conflict I can't resolve.

*[exeunt]*

---

**Contact Juggling!** *Glasses are the windows to the eyes, which are the doorways to your soul. If you need glasses but your character doesn't, you may need to wear contacts onstage. Also, if you <u>don't</u> need glasses but your character wears contacts, you may need to wear contacts onstage. If you need contacts and your character <u>also</u> needs contacts, you may not wear the same prescription. Remember, there are no "wrong" choices in the theatre, and the most difficult choices are always the most interesting. Try one eye with your character's prescription and one eye with yours, or swap them out halfway through. You'll need sharp eyes to gobble up all that attention!*

**T. I. P. S.**

# DON'T GET TRUNDLE POPPED

*For: Mean-mugged male, 13 years of age or older.*

 **TOUGH** *can be hard for actors, which is ironically tough in and of itself! Theatre kids are usually at the receiving end of bullying, so do a very advanced reverse projection and pretend to talk down to yourself! Flex your teeth and grit your muscles. You're hangin' tough!*

*[Author's note: Other monologue books have embarrassingly outdated slang that will make you look like a real wiener. The only way to make slang evergreen is to invent an entirely new vo-slang-ulary. This monologue has no expiration date!]*

It was never my choice to roll with a gang, I got ported into it. I can't just go around with my biff exposed, every young crone from here to 87th street will fork a lump just to see my inside ketchup.

You gotta get hopped into it, like everyone else. Hop in, hop out. The Stork Boys saw me gribble down the street one day. There was nine of them, they were all dressed the same, kippered shoes and triangle sleeves. I tried to look like I was minding my own to-do's, but the second they saw me fletch, they were all around me. The biggest one tells me to stop in my tramples. He pulls out a long thorn, holds it right to my chin. He says I look like I got some chip in my hip, thinks I could make Stork.

Before I could say anything, BAP, I take a frampton right to the ear, and fall right on my biff. What a way to start a friendship, right? Then I'm on the ground, and they're hitting me with everything: Paunches, flat gourds, minch sticks. Didn't even know what they were at the time, I had to figure it out from the bruises.

*[takes a long stare at the audience, they're not as tough as him]*

All of a supple, a pork slapper pulls me to my feet. Biggest one says I passed the test just by staying alive. He says I'm part of the family now, a Second Cousin if there ever was one. So now I'm one of them, part of the wobble, and we go everywhere together. The Morp Center, Laxxy's, The Plunkhole. Every shop, bar, and slip shack knows who we are and gives us respect. It's all about respect, that and bein' tough. Scone tough.

Sure, we'll have a wrinkle with another gang if they knuckle the line, but that's not what it's about. Out here on the streets, it's taint or be tainted. Everyone wants safety, respect, nobody wants to get glonked on their tramples home. Nobody wants their maternity ward getting a call that they got trundle popped just for skazzing when they should have ribbled. So when you see us, you better move your biff or I'll be the first one to take a long thorn to your neck. And that's not a threat, that's a glorkus.

*[exeunt]*

**Accents: Not Just for Home Decor Anymore!**
*If you read Harry Potter and didn't blink an eye at the stray U in colour, you can probably already pull off a British accent! If you hated the way Pepe Le Pew talked to female cats accidentally painted to look like skunks, but LOVED the way it sounded, go French! If you can roll an R or add an O to any word, you're practically speaking Spanish! Geez, that was easy!*

**T. I. P. S.**

# BABIES DON'T GIVE THEMSELVES UP

*For: Fertile-looking female, 15 years of age, who can play 30 using a cane and gray wig*

> **PROUD** – *You might not have accomplished enough in life to know what pride feels like, that's okay. Take one measure of ropeful, a swig of righteous, and a sprinkle of mischievous, and that's basically proud. Also, keep in mind you just read through a whole book! That's something to be proud of!*

Giving up my baby was the hardest thing I've ever done. I was only fifteen, scared out of my mind. I don't even know how it happened, my period was synced up with my sister, and *she* didn't get pregnant. Who knows. Anyway, this thing came out of me, a little creature full of love and burps and snot. I knew I couldn't take care of him. I thought, maybe there was a couple out there who needed a baby more than I did. A sweet, loving couple who couldn't make their own baby because their crotches didn't work. *[pats crotch mournfully]*

I thought about my baby, taking his first steps, learning to read, waiting in line for tickets to a Star Wars movie. I knew he wouldn't remember me, wouldn't know my face or hear me sing a lullaby. It tore me up, but I knew he'd have a better life. So I brought him here, to the adoption agency. *[waving arms to indicate entire room]* And they found a couple in no time. I signed the papers, handed my baby over, and I never even asked what was wrong with their crotches. It was the most mature thing I've ever done.

And you know what? I felt proud of myself, really really proud. All my friends said I was brave and fierce and glowing. They even had a baby shower for me, no baby. Can you believe it? I got so many gift cards, they couldn't even fit in my purse! My boyfriend Aiden was so cool about it. He said I made the right decision, and he never said that before! It was the best few weeks of my life, and I never wanted it to end. So I had another baby, a girl this time. Giving her up was the second hardest thing I've ever had to do.

I thought about her playing with dolls, getting makeovers, waiting in line for the bathroom. I knew these were things I couldn't ever hope to give her. So I brought her here, and they found another couple. Two gay guys who couldn't have a baby even if they tried! I thought, this is perfect, they're probably really good at makeup. It was still a lot of paperwork, but I got that super proud feeling again knowing she'd have a better life. It was like a fairy tale, but then...

Well, giving up my third baby was the third hardest thing I've ever done. This time, at least I knew where to find good parking. You know, on Chapman street, near the overpass? Aiden was super supportive, he said he was starting to get worried about me. Little old me! I told him to shut up and hop to it, so we could get to work on number four. It just kept getting easier! I helped so, so many babies find a better life. Twenty babies with twenty better lives, even more if you count all the twins separately. I just love the adoption process, it's the only game where everyone wins!

Now I'm thirty years old, practically an old maid. The funny thing is, now MY crotch is busted! *[pats crotch mournfully]* Would you believe it? And after all these years of giving, I'm finally ready to think about me. I've put myself through so much, it's high time *I'm* the one who gets a better life. So I'm putting *myself* up for adoption this time. Let's get started on that paperwork!

*[exeunt]*

# ABOUT THE AUTHOR

**Mike Levine** is the author of *Oh, the Flesh You Will Eat!* and this
is his second book written in the voice of a deranged and isolated
character. Originally from Oakland, California, Levine grew weary of
the theatre scenes in New York and Chicago before finally moving to
Los Angeles. He is a regular contributor to *The Onion,* and has written
Fantastic Four fanfiction for *Heeb Magazine* and "An Open Letter to
Busta Rhymes" for *McSweeney's.*

He likes to think teenagers taught him drama at the High School
Writer's Workshop at Sarah Lawrence College and California Acting
Workshop at UC Berkeley.

He also has way too many feelings.